How t
Rosary for Children

with Color Art Masterpieces for the 20 Mysteries

Kathryn Marcellino, OCDS

Abundant Life Publishing

How to Pray the Rosary for Children
with Color Art Masterpieces for the 20 Mysteries

by Kathryn Marcellino, OCDS

Abundant Life Publishing
PO Box 3753, Modesto, CA 95352
email: kathryn@abundantlifepublishing.com
www.AbundantLifePublishing.com

13-digit ISBN: 978-1-944158-07-1

Printed in the U.S.A.

About the Author: Kathryn Marcellino is an author, graphic designer, and the
mother of five grown children and a number of grandchildren. She is a member
of the Secular Order of Discalced Carmelites (OCDS) and has a graduate certificate
in Formation in Spiritual Theology. She is also a trained spiritual director with a
website at CatholicSpiritualDirection.org where she offers an e-mail newsletter
and an online course entitled "Seeking Union with God".

Kathryn Marcellino's other books include:
How to Pray the Rosary as a Pathway to Contemplation, Third Edition...
Twenty Mysteries of the Rosary Coloring Book...
Christian Cathedrals Stained Glass Coloring Book...
Jesse Tree Ornaments: Advent Coloring Activities and Craft Projects...
Saint Quotes on Love Catholic Meditations Coloring Book...
Art Extensions Christian Art Masterpieces Drawing and Coloring Book...

The Rosary, a Bible-Based Prayer

The prayers and events of the mysteries of the Rosary are mainly taken from the Bible. Jesus taught his apostles the Our Father (Matthew 6:5-13). The Hail Mary begins with the Angel Gabriel's words to Mary announcing that she was chosen to be the mother of Jesus Christ. "Hail, full of grace, the Lord is with you!" (Luke 1:28). The second sentence of the Hail Mary was addressed to Mary by her cousin Elizabeth, who exclaimed, "Blessed are you among women, and blessed is the fruit of your womb!" (Luke 1:42). The Apostles' Creed summarizes the teachings and beliefs of the Apostles.

Meditating on the Mysteries of the Rosary

Before beginning to pray, it is good to remember that we are in the presence of God and to whom we are speaking. Praying the Rosary is not merely saying vocal prayers but lifting our hearts and minds to God and meditating on the mysteries. The mysteries of the Rosary cover important events in the lives of Jesus and his mother Mary. While saying the 10 Hail Marys in a decade, we meditate or think about the mystery for that decade. Our Lady of Fatima taught seven-year-old Jacinta how to meditate on the mysteries of the Rosary by forming images of the mysteries in her mind as she prayed the Hail Marys.

The Joyful Mysteries are about Jesus's conception, birth, and childhood, and are usually said on Mondays and Saturdays. The Luminous Mysteries are about Jesus's public ministry and are usually said on Thursdays. The Sorrowful Mysteries are about Jesus's suffering and death, and are usually said on Tuesdays and Fridays. The Glorious Mysteries are about events after Jesus's death and are usually said on Sundays and Wednesdays.

How to Say the Rosary

6. Say the "Glory Be", (Optional Fatima Prayer), Announce 2nd Mystery, Say the "Our Father".

7. Say ten "Hail Marys".

8. Say the "Glory Be", (Optional Fatima Prayer), Announce 3rd Mystery, Say the "Our Father".

5. Say ten "Hail Marys".

4. Say the "Glory Be", (Optional Fatima Prayer), Announce 1st Mystery, Say the "Our Father".

9. Say ten "Hail Marys".

3. Say three "Hail Marys".

2. Say the "Our Father".

10. Say the "Glory Be", (Optional Fatima Prayer), Announce 4th Mystery, Say the "Our Father".

14. End with "Glory Be", (Optional Fatima Prayer), "Hail Holy Queen", and Optional Ending Prayers

13. Say ten "Hail Marys".

11. Say ten "Hail Marys".

1. Make the "Sign of the Cross", say the "Apostles' Creed".

12. Say the "Glory Be", (Optional Fatima Prayer), Announce 5th Mystery, Say the "Our Father".

Ideas for Praying with Children

It's optimal for each child to have their own rosary. One idea is to let the children take turns lighting a special candle to get their attention and then blowing it out at the end of prayer. It is easier to focus if the lights are off, a candle burning, and everyone is praying. If saying the entire rosary is too much at first, start with just one decade. Children often have concerns so invite them to add their intentions. The children might like to take turns leading a decade. For each decade, show them the picture in this book for the mystery, read the description, and perhaps read the Scripture reference. The more we know about God, the more we will love God and want to do what he asks. When teaching children about the reasons we pray the rosary include stories about Marian apparitions like Fatima, so they will better understand. These are just a few ideas, so experiment to find what works for you. The goal is for children to learn and want to pray as a positive experience.

The Prayers of the Rosary

Sign of the Cross: In the name of the Father, and of the Son and of the Holy Spirit. Amen.

Apostles' Creed: I believe in God, the Father almighty, Creator of heaven and earth, and in Jesus Christ, his only Son, our Lord, who was conceived by the Holy Spirit, born of the Virgin Mary, suffered under Pontius Pilate, was crucified, died and was buried; he descended into hell; on the third day he rose again from the dead; he ascended into heaven, and is seated at the right hand of God the Father almighty; from there he will come to judge the living and the dead. I believe in the Holy Spirit, the holy Catholic Church, the communion of saints, the forgiveness of sins, the resurrection of the body, and life everlasting. Amen.

Our Father: Our Father, who art in heaven, hallowed be thy name; thy kingdom come; thy will be done on earth as it is in heaven. Give us this day our daily bread; and forgive us our trespasses as we forgive those who trespass against us; and lead us not into temptation, but deliver us from evil. Amen.

Hail Mary: Hail Mary, full of grace, the Lord is with you; blessed are you among women, and blessed is the fruit of your womb, Jesus. Holy Mary, Mother of God, pray for us sinners now and at the hour of our death. Amen.

Glory Be: Glory be to the Father, the Son, and the Holy Spirit; as it was in the beginning, is now, and ever shall be, world without end. Amen.

Optional Fatima Prayer: Oh my Jesus, forgive us our sins, save us from the fires of hell; lead all souls to heaven, especially those most in need of Your Mercy.

Hail Holy Queen (Salve Regina): Hail, holy Queen, mother of mercy, our life, our sweetness, and our hope. To you do we cry, poor banished children of Eve; to you do we send up our sighs, mourning and weeping in this valley of tears. Turn, then, most gracious advocate, your eyes of mercy toward us; and after this, our exile, show unto us the blessed fruit of your womb, Jesus. O clement, O loving, O sweet Virgin Mary. Amen.

Optional Ending Prayers: Pray for us, O holy Mother of God that we may be made worthy of the promises of Christ. Let us pray. O God, whose Only Begotten Son, by his life, death, and resurrection, has purchased for us the rewards of eternal life, grant, we beseech thee, that meditating upon these mysteries of the most holy Rosary of the Blessed Virgin Mary, we may imitate what they contain and obtain what they promise, through the same Christ Our Lord. Amen.

The 20 Mysteries of the Rosary

1st Joyful Mystery:
The Annunciation

The Annunciation by Bartolome Esteban Murillo, 1655-1660

When Mary was a teenager, the Angel Gabriel appeared to her and said, "Hail, full of grace, the Lord is with you." (Luke 1:28) The angel announced to Mary that she was highly favored and that God had chosen her to be the mother of the Messiah. The angel also said that this would happen through the Holy Spirit. The angel told her to name her son, "Jesus", meaning Savior. Mary replied, "Behold, I am handmaid of the Lord. Let it be to me according to your word" (Luke 1:38). (If you'd like to read more of the story in the Bible, see Luke 1:26-38.)

2nd Joyful Mystery:
The Visitation

Mary's Visit to Elizabeth by Frans Francken the Younger, 1618

When the Angel Gabriel appeared to Mary, he also told her that her cousin Elizabeth was going to have a baby in her old age. Elizabeth's baby would be known as John the Baptist and would help prepare people for the coming of Jesus. Mary went to visit Elizabeth, who said to Mary, "Blessed are you among women, and blessed is the fruit of your womb," (Luke 1:42), which is the second sentence of the Hail Mary prayer. Mary stayed with Elizabeth for about three months and then returned home. (See Luke 1:39-60.)

3rd Joyful Mystery:
The Nativity

Adoration of the Christ Child by Lorenzo Lotto, 1523

When it was almost time for Jesus to be born, Mary and her husband Joseph, were required by law to travel to Bethlehem for a census. When they arrived, there were no rooms available for them, so they stayed in a stable or cave for animals. While there, Mary gave birth to the Baby Jesus and laid him in a manger. We call the day Jesus was born, Christmas. The angels appeared to shepherds in the field nearby. The angels sang praises to God and told the shepherds that a Savior had been born who is Christ the Lord. The shepherds hurried to see Baby Jesus and found him lying in a manger. (See Luke 2:1-16.)

7

4th Joyful Mystery:
The Presentation in the Temple

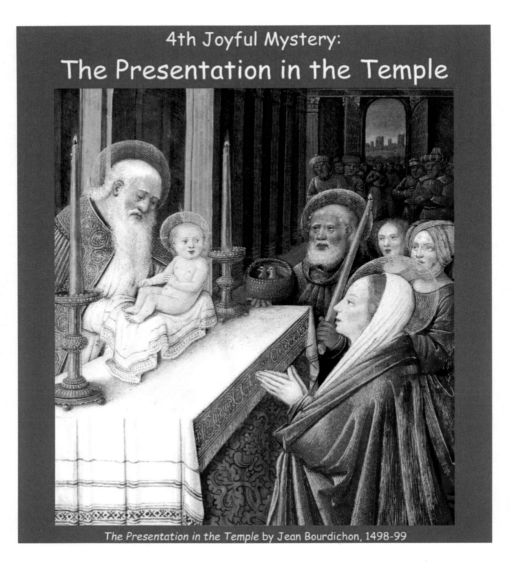

The Presentation in the Temple by Jean Bourdichon, 1498-99

Forty days after Jesus was born, Joseph and Mary took Jesus to the temple in Jerusalem for Mary's ritual purification after childbirth and to present Jesus as her firstborn in obedience to the Law of Moses. While they were there, the Holy Spirit informed the devout Simeon that Jesus was the Messiah. Simeon took Jesus in his arms and gave praise and thanks to God for allowing him to see the Messiah. Simeon told Mary that her child was set for the falling and rising of many in Israel, and that she would have much to suffer. An elderly prophetess named Anna was also in the Temple offering prayers and thanks to God for Jesus. She told everyone there about Jesus. (See Luke 2:22-33.)

5th Joyful Mystery:
The Finding of Jesus in the Temple

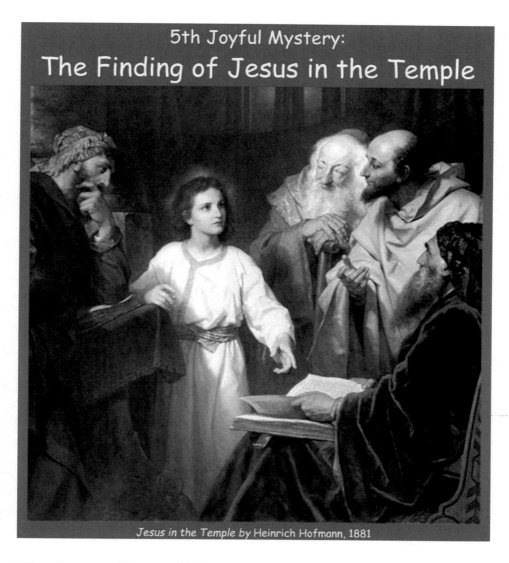

Jesus in the Temple by Heinrich Hofmann, 1881

When Jesus was 12 years old, he went with his parents to Jerusalem to celebrate the feast of the Passover. On the way back home, Mary and Joseph couldn't find Jesus anywhere. They looked for him for three days and finally found him in the Temple talking to the teachers who were amazed about how much Jesus knew about God. Mary and Joseph asked Jesus why he had stayed behind without telling them, as they had been worried. He said, "How it is that you sought me? Did you not know that I must be in my Father's house?" (Luke 2:49). His parents didn't seem to understand right away. Even though Jesus was the Son of God, he returned home with his parents and was obedient to them. His mother Mary thought about all these things and kept them in her heart. (See Luke 2:40-51.)

1st Luminous Mystery:
The Baptism of the Lord

The Baptism of Christ by Bartolomé Esteban Murillo, 1655

When Jesus was around 30 years old, it was time for him to leave his parents' house and teach the people. John the Baptist had helped prepare the people for Jesus's coming by "preaching a baptism of repentance for the forgiveness of sins" (Mark 1:4). John called people to repent, which means to be sorry for their sins and to stop sinning. John told the people that he was not the Christ, and his mission was to get things ready for Jesus. When Jesus went down to the Jordan River, he asked John to baptize him. When John baptized Jesus, the heavens opened up and the Holy Spirit descended upon Jesus like a dove. A voice from heaven said, "Thou art my beloved Son; with thee I am well pleased." (See Mark 1: 1-11.)

2nd Luminous Mystery:
The Wedding Feast at Cana

The Wedding Feast at Cana by Julius Schnorr von Carolsfeld, 1819

Mary, Jesus, and his disciples were attending a wedding when the party ran out of wine. Mary wanting to help said to Jesus, "They have no wine." (John 2:2) Even though Jesus said it was not yet time to reveal his power to the world, Mary told the servants, "Do whatever he tells you" (John 2:5). Jesus ordered the servants to fill six stone water jars with water and to take some of it to the head waiter. After tasting it, the head waiter told the bridegroom that while most people serve the best wine first, they had saved the best wine for last. This was the first miracle or sign Jesus performed revealing his power as the Son of God. His disciples believed in him. Jesus performed many other miracles later. (See John 2:1-11.)

3rd Luminous Mystery:
The Proclamation of the Kingdom

The Sermon on the Mount by Carl Bloch, 1877

When Jesus was about 30 years old, he went out to teach the people and proclaim the Gospel. (Gospel means "good news.") The good news is that the kingdom of God is at hand and that Jesus came that people might have eternal life. Jesus told people what God wanted them to do and how they should live. He said to believe in God, to stop sinning, and to ask for forgiveness. He told them to have faith in him, to obey God's commandments, and to love God and their neighbor. He worked miracles to show people that he was God, including healing the sick and raising the dead. (See Mark 1:15, Mark 2:3-12, Luke 7:47-48, and John 20:22-23.)

4th Luminous Mystery:
The Transfiguration

The Transfiguration by Raphael, 1516-1520

Jesus went up a high mountain with three of his apostles, Peter, James, and John. While there, Jesus's face shone like the sun, and his clothes became as white as light. Moses and Elijah were talking with him. From a cloud a voice said, "This is my beloved Son, with whom I am well pleased, listen to him" (Matthew 7:5). The apostles, filled with awe, fell down on the ground. When they looked up, they only saw Jesus, who told them not to tell anyone what they had seen until he had risen from the dead. This event showed them that they should listen to Jesus, who is above the Law of Moses and the prophets like Elijah. (See Matthew 17:1-9.)

5th Luminous Mystery:
The Institution of the Eucharist

Last Supper by Jaume Huguet, circa 1470

The night before Jesus died, he had his last supper with his apostles. It was on the Jewish feast of Passover when a lamb was slain and eaten in remembrance of God and Moses bringing the Israelites out of slavery in Egypt. At every Mass, Jesus is called the "Lamb of God, who takes away the sin of the world" (John 1:29). In the Old Testament, animal sacrifices were offered to make up for sin. However, the sacrifice that Jesus made by dying on the cross made up for all the sins of the entire world. After Jesus's perfect sacrifice of himself, there wasn't a need for any more animal sacrifices. When Jesus said to the apostles, "Do this in remembrance of me" (Luke 22:19), he instituted the sacrament of the Eucharist also called Holy Communion. Jesus desires to be united in communion with us. He loves us and wants us to love him in return and to love one another. (See Matthew 26:17-30.)

1st Sorrowful Mystery:
The Agony in the Garden

Christ in Gethsemane by Heinrich Hofmann, 1890

Right after having his last supper with the apostles, Jesus went to the Garden of Gethsemane to pray. While there he took upon himself all the sins of the world. He was suffering so much that "his sweat became like great drops of blood falling upon the ground" (Luke 22:44). He was with Peter, James, and John. He asked them to stay awake for an hour and pray. Jesus knew he would soon suffer and die on the cross to make up for all the sins of the world. He prayed three times to his Father in heaven to not have endure this, but he also prayed that the Father's will be done rather than his own will. Each time he went to see his apostles, he found the apostles sleeping. An angel came from heaven to help strengthen Jesus. Today the "holy hour" devotion comes from Jesus's request to his apostles to spend an hour with him in prayer. (See Matthew 26:36-46.)

2nd Sorrowful Mystery:
The Scourging at the Pillar

The Flagellation of Our Lord Jesus Christ by William-Adolphe Bouguereau, 1880

After Jesus prayed in the Garden of Gethsemane, a crowd came with swords and clubs, and arrested him. They took him to the high priest, and they asked if he was the Messiah, the Son of God. Jesus said that he was. The chief priests and elders didn't believe he was God's Son and accused him of blasphemy, which means being disrespectful to God or claiming to be God. In the morning, they handed him over to the Roman ruler, Pontius Pilate. Pilate asked Jesus if he really was the King of the Jews. Jesus said that his Kingdom was not of this world. This disturbed Pilate. He didn't want to be responsible for putting Jesus to death, so Pilate let the crowd decide what to do with Jesus, and they shouted to crucify him. Pilate had Jesus cruelly whipped. (See John 18:28-40, 19:1.)

3rd Sorrowful Mystery:
The Crowning with Thorns

Ecce Homo by Bartolome Esteban Murillo, 17th century

After Jesus was whipped and scourged, the soldiers ridiculed him. They took off his clothes and put a royal purple cloak on him and a crown of thorns on his head. They made fun of him and said, "Hail, King of the Jews!" (Matthew 27:29). They struck his head with a stick to torture him. They spat on him and knelt down to pretend to do him homage to humiliate him. Pilate brought Jesus out before the crowd again in the purple cloak and said, "Here is the Man!" (John 19:5). Pilate said that he found no fault in Jesus, but the crowd shouted, "Crucify him." (See Mark 15:6-20.)

The Carrying of the Cross

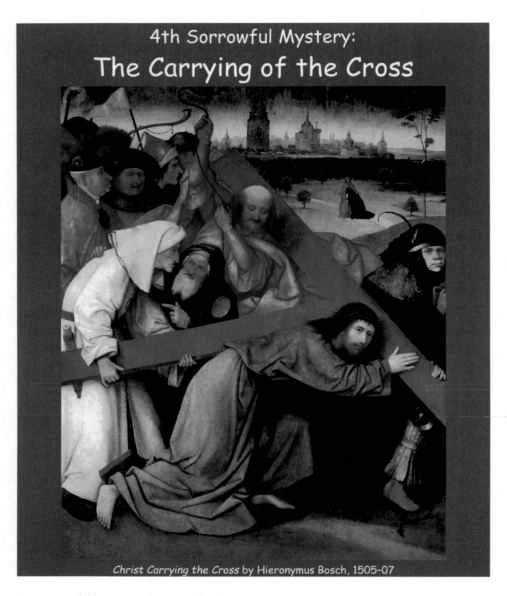

Christ Carrying the Cross by Hieronymus Bosch, 1505–07

Jesus was led away to be crucified and made to carry his cross. At one point, the soldiers forced a man named Simon of Cyrene to help him carry the cross. People were following Jesus, and some women were crying. According to tradition, one women named Veronica wiped Jesus's face with her veil and a miracle took place. A picture of Jesus's face was left on her veil. (See Luke 23:13-28.)

The Crucifixion

Crucifixion by Andrea Previtali, circa 1500s

When they arrived at Mount Calvary, the soldiers stripped Jesus of his clothes and nailed him to the cross. Jesus was offered wine mixed with gall to drink. He was crucified between two thieves. According to Mark's Gospel, Jesus hung on the cross for about six hours from nine in the morning until his death at about three in the afternoon. The soldiers put a sign on the cross above his head, which said, "Jesus of Nazareth, King of the Jews" in three languages (John 19:19). They divided his garments and cast lots for his robe. The soldiers did not break Jesus's legs as they did to the other two crucified men. A soldier thrust a lance into his side, and blood and water flowed out showing that Jesus was dead. Then they buried him. (See Luke 23:33-49.)

1st Glorious Mystery:
The Resurrection

Resurrection by Carl Heinrich Bloch, 1873

After death, Jesus's body was wrapped in a linen cloth and buried. On the third day, he rose from the dead. The day that Jesus came back to life is called Easter. On the first Easter Sunday, Mary Magdalene and another Mary visited the tomb. They found the stone rolled back. Jesus's body was missing, and they saw an angel who said, "He is not here; for he has risen, as he said." (Matthew 28:6). Later Jesus appeared to Mary Magdalene and told her to tell the apostles what she had seen. (John 20:11-18). After coming back to life, Jesus appeared many times to the apostles and others. (See Matthew 28:1-20.)

2nd Glorious Mystery:
The Ascension

The Ascension by John Singleton Copley, 1775

One evening after Jesus rose from the dead, he appeared to the disciples and said, "Peace be with you." He showed them his hands, feet, and side. The disciples were very happy to see him. Jesus said to them, "As the Father has sent me, even so I send you." He breathed on them and said, "Receive the Holy Spirit. If you forgive the sins of any, they are forgiven; if you retain the sins of any, they are retained" (from John 20:19-23). Jesus instituted the Sacrament of Reconciliation, also called Confession. Jesus appeared many other times and performed many other signs as well. One day, he told the apostles that they would be baptized with the Holy Spirit soon. Then Jesus was lifted up in a cloud and went to heaven. Two men with white robes told the disciples that Jesus would come again from Heaven on a cloud. This event is called the Second Coming, which will happen in the future at the end of the world. (See Acts 1:1-11.)

3rd Glorious Mystery:
The Descent of the Holy Spirit

Pentecost by El Greco, 1597

After Jesus went up to Heaven, the apostles went back to Jerusalem and spent their time in prayer. On Pentecost, they were gathered in one place and heard a loud noise like a strong wind. Then, what looked like tongues of fire came to rest on each of them, and they were filled with the Holy Spirit. Many people from various places were in Jerusalem that day, and the people heard the apostles speak about Jesus in their own language. Peter said, "Repent, and be baptized every one of you in the name of Jesus Christ for the forgiveness of your sins; and you shall receive the gift of the Holy Spirit" (Acts 2:38). About 3,000 people were baptized that day. Pentecost is often called the birthday of the Church. (See Acts 2:1-38.)

4th Glorious Mystery:
The Assumption of Mary

The Assumption of the Virgin by Bartolomé Esteban Murillo, 1670

Mary was honored by God to be the mother of Jesus Christ, the Savior of the world. God created Mary without the stain of Original Sin on her soul because she would be the mother of Jesus. This is called the Immaculate Conception. She lived a very holy life doing all that God asked of her. When it was time for Mary to die, both her body and soul were taken up to Heaven to be with God. Based on the longstanding tradition of the church, Pius XII infallibly defined the Assumption of Mary body and soul into heaven as a dogma of faith in 1950. (See 1 Corinthians 15:13-18 and *Catechism of the Catholic Church #966.*)

5th Glorious Mystery:
The Coronation of Mary

The Coronation of the Virgin by Diego Velazquez, 1600s

When Mary arrived in Heaven, she was crowned as the Queen of Heaven. She is a Queen because she is the mother of Jesus, who is called King because he is our Savior and the Son of God. She is not only a Queen, but since we are baptized children of God, she is also our spiritual mother in Heaven who loves us very much and intercedes for us with her Son Jesus. (See Luke 1:46-49 and *Ad Caeli Reginam: Encyclical of Pope Pius XII on Proclaiming the Queenship of Mary.*)